Gail & Me

Written by Virginia King
Illustrated by Margaret Power

For a long time it was just Dad, Terry, and me. We used to call ourselves "the three men." I liked that — I could pretend that I was a man already.

Dad had to learn to cook and do the wash and things like that. He started doing all those things while Mom was still in the hospital. He even went to microwave cooking classes.

It was great when he made his first microwave chocolate cake.

We told Mom all about it, and she laughed and cried all at the same time. I was only little then, so I didn't really understand why she did that.

When Mom died (I was only four),
we were kind of used to being the three
men already. Not that it made it any easier.
We still missed her a lot. We still do, and
sometimes when I close my eyes I can see
her face as clearly as anything.

And I've still got her teddy bear, too.
He used to be mine, but I gave him to
Mom when she was in the hospital, so that
she'd have someone to hug if she got scared
at night. She called him Hugbert.

I'm too old for teddy bears now, but
sometimes Hugbert gets scared at night,
so I hug him, and I think of Mom.

I thought it would always be just the three of us, after Mom died. But then Dad met Gail.

We went to a party at a friend's house one night, and there she was. Dad always took us out with him. He hardly ever left us with a baby-sitter. Wherever he went, we went — the three men. I was glad about that. It meant I could make sure that nothing happened to him.

But even though I was with him on this night, something happened anyway.

Gail came over to our house all the time. Sometimes she even cooked dinner. But at least she didn't act like a mother — I mean, she didn't try to tell me what to do or anything.

Gail was always friendly. She asked me questions about school, and came out to talk to me while I was playing in the yard — things like that. I think she liked me and Terry, and I guess we liked her, but it wasn't the same as being the three men.

Every weekend Gail came over to our
house to visit, and whenever we went out,
Gail came with us. It was as if she was
part of our family, but she wasn't —
not really.

She and Dad hugged each other a lot.
They smiled and laughed a lot, too.
But Gail and I never hugged each other.
We just said hello and goodbye with our
arms by our sides. I was glad about that.
I got all the hugs I needed from Dad and
Hugbert.

Then one day we all went out for a picnic with a big group of people, and afterwards, when we were walking back to the car, I asked Gail if she was coming back to our house for dinner. (I knew she would be.)

She said, "Yes I am, Paul," and looked at me. I felt I had to say something, so I said, "Good."

Gail laughed and gave me a big hug — and I hugged her back!

Things were different after that. Gail
and I gave each other lots of hugs
whenever we said hello and goodbye, and
it felt good having her around. I forgot
about not being the three men anymore.

Then, one day, Gail and Dad asked
me and Terry to sit down — they said
they wanted to tell us something.

I knew what it was going to be and I
could feel my heart starting to thump.
It was okay giving Gail a hug, but I
didn't want anything else to happen.

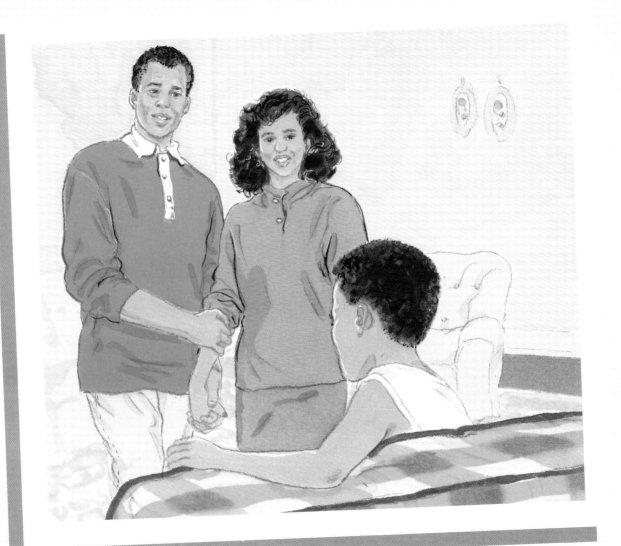

Dad looked serious and happy all at the same time. He said, "Gail and I have decided to get married."

I heard the words, but I didn't feel anything. Terry said, "That's cool," and went off to his room. "Cool?" It wasn't "cool" at all! What about Mom? I wasn't going to have Gail for a mom. I didn't need a mom. Dad was a perfectly good dad and mom. His microwave cakes were really great!

Tears were filling my eyes. I couldn't think of anything to say. Then Gail came over and put her arms around me, and I burst into tears. I didn't want to cry, but I couldn't help it.

Then she said, "You don't want a new mom, do you Paul?"

And I whispered, "No."

Gail said, "That's good. Your mother was a great mom, and I don't want to take her place."

I said, "But if you marry Dad, won't you be my mom?"

Gail said, "Not if you don't want it, and I don't. We can be friends, instead."

So Dad and my friend Gail got married. Terry and I got all dressed up for the wedding. Gail looked really beautiful and Dad looked really handsome. It was just like in the movies!

It's good living with Gail. She isn't my mom, but she helps Dad take care of Terry and me, and she helps me with my homework. Sometimes she cooks, and sometimes Dad cooks.

I went shopping with Gail yesterday.
The woman in the store looked at me
and she looked at Gail, and then she
said to Gail, "Is he your son?"

Gail smiled and said, "No."

So the woman asked, "Is he
your brother?"

And Gail said, "No."

Then Gail smiled at me,
and she turned to the
woman and said,
"He's my friend."